SERENDIPITY

Robert Witmer

Copyright© 2023 Robert Witmer
ISBN: 978-93-95224-52-9

First Edition: 2023
Rs. 200/-

Cyberwit.net
HIG 45 Kaushambi Kunj, Kalindipuram
Allahabad - 211011 (U.P.) India
http://www.cyberwit.net
Tel: +(91) 9415091004
E-mail: info@cyberwit.net

Printed at VCORE

Table of Contents

FOREWORD

Serendipity. Making happy and unexpected discoveries. It is my hope that this book provides the reader with plenty of opportunities for such discoveries.

The 4th century poet Tao Yuanming (better known in English as T'ao Ch'ien), wrote: "But he kept writing poems to amuse himself, and they show something of who he was." Wallace Stevens, in one of his last poems, "The Planet on the Table," expressed a similar notion:

> Ariel was glad he had written his poems.
> They were of a remembered time
> Or of something that he liked.

Like Tao and Stevens, I am happy that I have put into words something of myself and my experiences, and of the world in which I wandered and wondered. The sense of wonder keeps our eyes open. It allows us to see what is unfamiliar in the familiar. New insights derive from new perspectives, which find their coign of vantage in the mountains of mutability, where a liberating breeze blows away our arrogant assumptions and comfy certainties. For besides seeing what is beautiful in the world, we must also give attention to where we have gone wrong and what we might do to remedy those wrongs.

The words in this book have given me a way of thinking about things. They are, inadequate as they may be, intended to evoke in the reader an awareness and a sense of wonder at the beauty and bewilderments of the world, and the mystery of life.

My book is comprised of short poems (haiku and senryu) and haibun-like prose poetry, interspersed with quotations and brief comments. The quotations are there because someone else managed to say what I wanted to say better than I ever could. The material has been arranged into sections and sequences. However, although one might find interesting patterns in my arrangements, the reader should feel free to jump around from section to section and piece to piece as the spirit of the moment moves her. The haibun in the first section, The Road Before Me, are drawn from my travel experiences. The pieces are not intended to tell my life story but rather to tell stories of places and peoples and ways of living that I was fortunate enough to encounter along the way.

As I wrote at the end of the Foreword to my first book of poems, I agree with Wallace Stevens that "poetry is a search for happiness" and that "a poem should stimulate the sense of living and being alive." I hope that the pieces here bring a measure of that joy of life to you. The world is a marvelously complex place, and life is for living.

The Road Before Me

Life is a journey, and each step, regardless of direction, is a
step forward.

"If you walk your path without singing, you insult the land."
　　　— Estonian saying

"Never wait for yourself."
　　　— Paul Eluard and Benjamin Peret

"I felt no more the bargeman's guiding hands."
　　　— Arthur Rimbaud

"True seeing is an act of love."
　　　— George Oppen

Rain

Let the rain kiss you
Let the rain beat upon your head with silver liquid drops
Let the rain sing you a lullaby
          — Langston Hughes, "April Rain Song"

Noah was 600 years old when the windows of heaven opened. What are forty days of rain when one has lived that long. For me, eight days were enough. Cycling from Chicago to Clearwater, Florida, setting up my tent in the rain, packing it away in the rain, pushing slippery pedals through the rain, I was soaked to the bone. The rain had kissed me, it had sung to me, it had brought the very heavens down upon my head – but there appeared no dove with an olive leaf.

God moves in a mysterious way. These words, composed by William Cowper shortly before he attempted suicide by drowning, found their rhythm in a rainy night in Georgia, along a puddled highway, in the flickering light of a small motel, where I stopped and requested a room, only to be told all the rooms were taken, but one, which the kindly proprietor offered at half price, for there was a leak in the roof, somewhere over the bed. Deep down my soggy brain a still small voice whispered "it's all right," the flooded night should pass and I would place a pillow on my head and there the rain could beat its muffled tune.

When Tony Joe White wrote his now famous song he knew he had to write about something he knew. He knew a lot of rainy nights (and days too I suppose) and his song sold a million copies. I counted the raindrops that night in Georgia, like sheep, in the hope of slipping into a peaceful slumber. There may have been a million, none were missing. Researchers at Oxford University have found that imagining a waterfall might work as well as sheep – but, well, I had enough of water, and though I failed to pull the wool over my eyes, I took solace in the raindropped baptism of my relatively anhydrous pillowed cowl. I must have dreamed.

rain lifts the little boat
I trail my oars and let
the waters let me go

In the Lotus Sutra, the Buddha tells of the rain that falls on all plant life: It is the same rain for all, yet each grows in its own way. I had received my full share of rain, the heavens had watered me in accordance with my needs so that I might be lifted, joyous and exuberant, into the sun which shines, sooner or later, equally on all.

autumn rain
one deep breath
through a bamboo flute

The morrow came and the sun shone and my bicycle glistened in the doorway. The road stretched out before me, the earthly mud at its edges and its smooth surface gleaming in the open air. I rode on.

rain rinsed air
spilling sunlight
in the steady stream

Evening at Kastro's

The whitewashed wonder of Mykonos before the tourist
hordes.

Clear water clouds the ouzo, as beauty beguiles time.

Mozart's *Requiem* in vinyl turning round the still point of the
needle in its veins.

We make of metaphors a place to be another, which can never
be.

What youth enjoys and passes beyond, memory hoards away.

Sunset in the windmills by the sea.

> temple ruins
> a spring wind awakens
> marble curtains

Hospitality

"Your friends are here," the young Turk announces as he
approaches the backgammon table where Alex and I sit with
our new friends, sipping from fluted glasses tea spiked with
cognac, the consumption of which, it seems, is the usual
evening pastime for the men we joined when the driver of the
truck that carried us to this remote village stopped for the
night, gesturing toward the sole café as a place where we
might orient ourselves, which we managed to do without
much ado due to Alex's German fluency, a language also
spoken by one of the backgammon-playing, cognac-sipping
men, the man who seems to be in charge of things and in that
capacity has arranged for Alex and I to spend the night in the
local jail, as it contains two beds, presently unoccupied
according to the village policeman, who is also a part of our
merry company.

"What friends?" Alex and I wonder as we look incredulously
at each other. Here in a tiny village on a remote steppe at the
edge of the Anatolian plateau? We left our two friends that
morning when we began hitchhiking north from the sea at
Antalya. They were to follow later, by another route, and we
were all to meet up in a few days in Konya, where, in the 13th
century, Jelaluddin Rumi founded the whirling dervishes. But
presently, as fate would have it, our friends have been whirled
into the world of this Turkish village, where there are now too
many for the comfy confines of the jail.

With the new arrivals, our company disbands and, out of the
blue, we four foreigners are invited to spend the night at a
local family's home. My stay in jail would have to wait for
another day. We are given a room, a sumptuous dinner, and
then a boys' night out, to view a film at the village school
gymnasium, a rather risqué motion picture for this provincial
place, the hoots and whistles rising to a crescendo when the
celluloid couple finally kiss – on the lips!

Returned to our lodging, we sleep in a comfortably carpeted
and pillowed room, but come midnight I must pee, and so I
make my way to the toilet, and in so doing pass another room,
smaller, where all the members of the extended family are

11

sleeping, huddled together under what few blankets remain. With morning, there is breakfast – yoghurt, coffee, bread – and then a tour of the village, a Q&A, and a footrace with a local lad. Finally, the promised bus to Konya and our departure to the well wishes of our hosts. The journey continues, through Turkey and beyond. Through time.

And then . . . a handful of memories. Lives re-lived in the hospitality of words.

The tale told, I check my email – a message from abroad: Another friend at death's door.

> darkness fills the room
> the knock of a clock
> time's steady pendulum

Farouk's

a self returning mostly memory
— Wallace Stevens, "Anglais Mort à Florence"

Farouk's. The world was different then. Ignorance was bliss –
for the ignorant. Kabul was peaceful, the markets were full of
fruit, and the cool nights resounded with music: dambura,
tabla, and, sometimes, a friend's flute. Young travelers came
and went, like the summer days. And then, for no particular
reason, it was time to go – to journey to the east, with every
intention to return.

Each day the sun returns on its journey from east to west –
from Tokyo to Farouk's. But there is no Farouk's. A war has
seen to that. The climate has changed. White hair covers and
thins over troubled thoughts, like snow melting in the Hindu
Kush. One nears the end when the hoard of memory
attenuates, and one struggles to utter the ineffable images of
time and consciousness in the vain and hopeless effort to
complete a picture of life.

> ebb tide
> from our vanishing footprints
> to the setting sun

to have come all this way
to find nothing but distance
— from a poem by Li Ho, translated by David Young

The Woman in Leh

The lens was about as long as the barrel of a sawed-off
shotgun – aimed straight at her deeply wrinkled face. The
tourist must have had an itchy trigger finger, for she snapped
off one shot after another. Perhaps this jewel thief managed to
land a few rounds where the old woman's tears fell outside the
frame.

Of course, in a work of art some exaggeration is allowable.
She wasn't a jewel thief in the same sense as Alain Delon in
Le Cercle Rouge; she was simply interested in taking home
some photographs of a Ladakhi *perak*, the headdress covered
in turquoise that was once a symbol of aristocracy.

Tibetan turquoise, the product of snowmelt gone underground,
is a luxury item, on sale in any shop in Leh. Each piece is
unique in its patterning, no different in that way from the
pattern of wrinkles in a person's face. For the people who live
in the Himalayas these "Sky Stones" have spiritual value.
Their blue-green color brings heaven to earth. They have long
been used as a token of love that protects both giver and
receiver.

The good traveler takes only photographs and leaves only
footprints. Jean-Pierre Melville took the title of his heist film
from the Buddha, who drew a *cercle rouge* and said, "When
men, even unknowingly, are to meet one day, whatever may
befall each, whatever diverging paths, on the said day, they
will inevitably come together in a red circle."

> turquoise talisman
> the heaven we can buy
> ground to the bone

Benares

What to make of memories of death. Twice gone. And yet the
light in the temple by the holy river and the dirge of the
harmonium go on. Antyesti: The body burned in final
sacrifice. Go to the waters the scriptures say. Cold ashes fall
into the holy river, where they flow away to the sea, the gold
in the teeth caught in an untouchable's wicker basket. What
remains. Untouched. By death. Or music's memories. Of light
at night. A river of dead stars shining overhead. Even life
when one was young. Was old. The gods made the river. We
made it holy. With our ashes, our music, our gold teeth, and
our memories.

> moonlight
> on a passing river
> love trembles

Smoke and Mirrors

We talk about the films of Kurosawa, and Satyajit Ray. He knows them all, this self-professed young sadhu, my age, long ago. We are sitting cross-legged on the marble floor of a small temple, overlooking the Ganges, at Rishikesh, not far, but on the other side, from the ashram where the Beatles studied transcendental meditation, their graffiti still visible on the crumbling walls that must in some other dimension resonate with the songs they played between asanas.

We smoke charas, and mischief-maker that I am, I say: You smoke as you say Lord Shiva smoked, yet the Great Yogi inhaled but a single drop of sacred nectar, and that to save the universe from darkness. This is our third chillum. He smiles an eternal smile and replies: *There is so much more wrong with this world of ours.*

      braiding the smoke's dark hair bodhi tree

Goats

Goats. One of the oldest domesticated animals on Earth, descending from the bezoar ibex of the Zagros Mountains. Notorious for escaping their pens. They have a capacity for communication with human beings, though that has not always been favorable, as the goateed devil was wont to whisper lewd phrases in the ears of the saints.

In early spring kids spring onto the low stone walls in the hallowed landscapes of the Greek isles, not far from the clubs and the beaches and the world people make to forget the world they've made. The spiritual light which dresses and undresses all things plays about these young goats in an inexpressible and penetrating way.

> butterflies feed blossoms
> while a boy with a net
> catches sunshine

It is cold in central Turkey in the spring. The hitchhiker's thumb is numb, the hitchhiker dumb when the driver thumbs him to the back of the truck. It's better than nothing to escape the cold. Or so he thinks, the poor scapegoat, who finds himself scrapping with hungry billies for space behind the wind-breaking cab. Rock hard heads and a proverbial stubbornness drive these Pan-lusted beasts to nibble his clothes, as the truck bounces between the folded mountains on the Anatolian Plateau.

But summer can be colder. From the bus that descends from the Zoji La he sees ahead long-haired goats pressing themselves against the stone wall of a shepherd's hut. It is Dras, the second coldest inhabited place in the world. The goats are motionless in the wind. But the bus rolls on toward Leh, and he sees more goats against an adjoining wall that now faces his window in the bus. These goats have a slightly better angle to the wind, the cold cold wind. And then he sees the third wall of the tumbled structure, opposite the blowing of the wind, where it is still cold and the goats are bigger, still against the wall. These goats are not alone. At the spot where the wind blows least is their shepherd. He is not the shepherd

17

that will not bless the goat at his left hand, but he will not relinquish his place against the wall.

While summer may be cold, so too may autumn be warm – even in the world's highest mountains, the majestic Himalayas. There on the original trail to Everest is Karantichap, a lovely little village with a magnificent peepal tree – where a goat stands on its most outstanding branch. Yes, goats climb trees. They are the only ruminant to do so. And when the villagers have hung the tree with wreaths of marigolds, the goat must climb to graze upon the sweet flowers in the holy bodhi tree.

This tree of awakening once greeted the trekker as he passed through the village of Karantichap. One majestic branch, the branch favored for marigold wreaths and hungry goats, reached across the square at the center of the village, offering shade and a place for one and all to sit and sip sweet tea and tell whatever tales one might tell. The branch was as long as the history of the village, but it is no more. On his return weeks later the trekker found that they had amputated the ancient limb to make a space to park a bus that would pass along the road that would be built through the mountains where the poor isolated villagers of Karantichap lived, where their ancestors had lived, together with their tree-climbing goats.

Gone now to memory, the limb and the spirit of the tree and the goat and the marigolds. Gone like the trail that passed through the village, where now, I suppose, a road with its buses goes by. Gone too are the goats in Dras, gone like the goats in the back of the truck passing through the Anatolian wind. Gone like the kids that sprung onto the wall. Like the wall between each moment and the next.

> snow falls
> an old monk
> sets aside his beads

Perspectives

He sipped his butter tea in a corner of the dark room. A poor peasant mother did her chores near the hearth, occasionally tugging a string that rocked her infant's cradle on the floor about midway between the trekker and the tug. A common situation on the Himalayan trail some 50 years ago.

What the Nepali woman saw as she stirred the pot. What the foreigner in his absentminded rest saw in that dingy room. What the thin chicken pecking at the dirt floor might have seen. The baby in the cradle with its eyes looking upward at the smoke.

The chicken hopped about, pecking, moving nearer to the cradle, which was covered with a blanket that was itself covered in dust and the regurgitations of the baby who rocked there peacefully. The mother cooked. The trekker watched. The chicken hopped up on the cradle and pecked. Pecking, pecking, slowly moving up the blanket, toward the baby's face.

If a tree falls in the forest and no one hears it, does it make a sound? Perhaps the sound of one hand clapping. Or the sound of a trekker's boot swiftly through the air, on its way toward a fated fowl.

The hero to a baby's eyes. A crazed outsider come to kill our eggs. The visitor could not explain the punted hen – its final squawk – the puff of dust in the yard beyond the open door – the feathers settling down around the lifeless bird. The mother at the hearth could only gasp. The baby cried.

> hearth smoke
> a thin chicken with one eye
> on the iron pot

Before the Monastery at Thyangboche

The mind empties. The mountain is there, behind other mountains. Everest, Sagarmatha, Chomolungma. A plume that is a cloud of snow blows from its peak. It is not a white flag. The mountain will not surrender to words. It appears, though once concealed by clouds, when the *puja* begins and the monks blow their long horns, their long deep haunting sound, like the singing of elephants, carrying outward and upward toward the highest peak, through a sky that turns pink and purple and gold as the clouds part and Everest emerges, just the peak, behind other mountains, waving a flag of snow that is snow but not a flag. Beyond words, the sound of the horns and the chanting of the monks, more sound than words, *Om Mane Padme Hum*, the bodhisattva of compassion. The mountain is of itself and makes itself an image in our minds, which makes an image of the mountain, which makes our minds, for one moment of magic, one mind.

> temple bell
> between the tolls
> the sound of snow

Thyangboche is the largest gompa in the Khumbu region. The structure was built in 1923. In 1934, it was destroyed by an earthquake but subsequently rebuilt. It was destroyed again by a fire in 1989, and again rebuilt. Everest rose with the Himalaya during the Cenozoic collision of India with Asia about 55 million years ago. It continues to rise, while its glacier, the highest in the world, retreats, having lost in the past 25 years ice that took 2000 years to form – a result of human-induced climate change. This rapid glacier melt, occurring across the Himalaya, threatens the water supply for more than one and a half million people. We cannot rebuild these glaciers.

Om Mani Padme Hum.

Langtang

It was better to start before the sun came up. It would be easier to walk on the snow.

We squirmed out of the tent to pack our things. Paw prints encircled the tiny tent – snow leopard tracks. The ghost of a ghost that silently passed in the night.

The tracks led the way we were to go – over the open snow to the trickle of an early spring stream. There they vanished.

> before the mountain
> the frozen waterfall
> where the river rests

Much adventure remained – a summit, a blizzard, lost for days without food, the treacherous descent from ice to raging river. We survived, as memories do – to be happy, to be troubled, unsure.

> a bird's nest
> when all the leaves are gone
> notes to a song

The Sightseer

Back and forth in her sari, the bricks she stacked one by one on the cloth round her head swaying ever so slightly, she ambles toward the low wall, where slowly she bends forward to drop, all together, the bricks on the sand, within easy grasp of the mason, who places them, one by one, into the design he carries in his head, now slowly forming in the courtyard of the Bayview Hotel. What was a desolate patch of sand will be a patio, for guests to sip their morning chai and their evening cocktails.

I have been watching since the work began early in the morning, thinking how inefficient this almost primitive approach to construction seems to be, assured in the comfortable familiarity of my own mind that I could do the job much better.

> a mechanical owl
> rotates his head to see
> the sound of a cuckoo clock

The sun rises higher over the sea and, in the increasingly blazing heat, the work goes on. Slowly but steadily, in an almost mystical harmony, the two silent laborers, the peasant in her yellow sari and the mason in his lungi, create the patio. Slowly too a little light shines through the shutters of my certainty.

By noon the job is done. It must be infernally hot where the new patio has now been placed, for I am sweating in the shade of the porch, where I sip my second mango lassi. This evening I will be able to drink and think a little nearer to the sea. Shutters open to a clear sky.

> cuckoo
> hidden among the leaves
> a song of spring

Outrigger

Now, in calm water, to swim in the open ocean is as easy to
the practiced swimmer as to ride in a spring-carriage ashore.
But the awful lonesomeness is intolerable. The intense
concentration of self in the middle of such heartless
immensity, my God! who can tell it?
— Herman Melville, *Moby Dick*

It must have been that sense of invulnerability that makes a
young man look just right for the lead in a Hollywood film
purged of the punitive response to hubris that an Olympian
ethos would necessitate that compelled him to sit on the spar
of the outrigger that lovely late tropical afternoon. A small
rented sailing boat crewed by two landlubbers light in the
wallet, lovers just right for a tipsy craft.

Eyes fixed on the crystal clear water that gave back his
handsome reflection, an echo of light that shimmered brighter
than the girl on the boat, he smiled like the tropical sun
warming his shoulders, lifting sparks through the splashes of
the South China Sea.

One rounded wave passed along the water and under the boat,
rocking it ever so slightly. A slip. To pass lightly, to go
quietly, carelessly, to steal imperceptibly, to fall or to sink,
and to lose one's command, overlooked, soon away.

How soon, how soon we move from the mystery of cause to
the clarity of consequence. Destiny, fate, a dome in the midst
of the waters and all that is good, and the darkness called
night.

Evening came upon the water and it was lonely in the South
China Sea. The awful essence of what is deeper than
understanding came to be seen in the mind's eye. It was seen,
it was of loneliness but it was not alone. It was of others who
lose what is lost and the terrible sense of their loss. This he
could not lose. His prayers were not for himself, they were for
them. For them he moved on the water and waited for . . .
what?

What returned from that miraculous salvation was another boat by happenstance to find the man alone in the middle of the darkness and the waves. The lovers were reunited and they loved. Life goes on, and mystery remains in the wondrous depths of the sea.

> a black wave
> crashes on the shore
> ten thousand stars

The Cave

A place of refuge. A place of eternal rest. Home to Calypso
and the Cyclops, the Sibyl and the King of the Winds. Where
Night hides during the day and Plato's shackled prisoners
undertake their ignorance for truth.

The earliest human fossils to be found in caves are probably
not the remains of those who lived there but rather of those
who were dragged into the caves by carnivores, to be
consumed in peace. With only a few exceptions, ancient
human beings never lived in caves, for they were damp and
dark, uneven and dangerous, home to lions and bears.
Eventually, however, our Paleolithic ancestors learned to
exploit these caverns as sanctuaries of the human spirit. Artist-
shamans squeezed themselves into chambers far underground
to engage their religious and symbolic preoccupations in a
dialogue with the rock walls, painting radiant frescoes of
bison, aurochs, and other creatures of the animal world of
which they saw themselves a part.

The adventurous spirit of these prehistoric artists does not
seem to have been dampened by fear of their fat-burning
lamps going out, leaving them alone in darkness more than a
kilometer from the entrance to their cave. They were occupied
with a gesture of harmony, an undertaking that elevated them
into a world of ideas and art.

Today people enter caves for the purpose of sightseeing. A
paradox, no? To enter willingly a place of darkness in order to
see. Nevertheless, one sunny day in the lovely town of Sagada
in the mountains of the island of Luzon in the Philippines, my
beloved and I ventured into Sumaguing Cave, the most
famous of the 60 caves discovered underneath the town. We
were guided by a kind young man, who led us through the
entrance and down, deeper and deeper into the cave. We
walked on wet limestone and wiggled through narrow
openings, the trail becoming steeper and slipperier as we went
along. We saw beautiful rock formations, stalactites and
stalagmites, and natural pools of ice cold water, lit by the
lantern carried by our guide.

bat cave
the feel of darkness
in the wet walls

The mantle of a lantern generates incandescent bright white light when heated by a flame. It is a fragile thing, brittle as the dust it becomes when, with the slightest shock, it crumbles and the light is gone. How dark is dark when the lantern strikes against wet rock and the light goes out? There is no natural light in the eternal darkness of the underworld. A cave is a natural void in the ground, and as such, it is not dissimilar to a grave – that dark realm which is no place to be, a void to avoid.

In an instant our cave became a place of transformation, a latent tomb, a subterranean sepulcher. Metamorphoses – the Earth's unending cycle of life, death, and – yes – rebirth. Like the Magdalenian artists of prehistoric times, our guide had brought along a survival kit, containing a spare mantle and the waterproof matches we needed to make it light. There would be a resurrection, and we would rise from the darkness back into the light of the sun, the Form of Goodness that shone in the bright blue sky above a small town in the mountains.

the newborn wakes
in mother's arms
sunbeams in a spring sky

Shikoku

Another day of cycling along the coast of Shikoku. Past a pack
of curious macaques – seeing, hearing, and speaking no evil –
I push on in the gloaming round the beautiful Ashizuri Misaki,
until, well after dark, I reach a tiny village by the sea.

I set up my tent on the beach and go in search of food. There
are no eateries I see, but there is a general store, closed it
seems, though a faint light is visible through the glass-
windowed doors.

I slide open one of the doors and call in a greeting. It's alright,
come in, a friendly voice replies – and so, with my foreign
face, helmet and odd-looking bicycling gloves, I enter and
peruse the aisles for snacks I might munch in my tent.
Sardines, peanuts, dried seaweed and a can of beer – that
should do the trick.

I make my way to the counter to pay, and call again to the
proprietor, who has, in that trusting Japanese village way, let
me roam the shop alone. She appears. Middle-aged, fresh from
the bath by the smell of things, smiling. She is wearing
something like a loose skirt, though I really don't see that
clearly, for she is naked from the waist up.

I remember those old National Geographics that my
adolescent friends and I would rifle through in the school
library, looking for the latest exposé from some exotic land
where the people have a rather different sense of modesty
from what we learn in Middle America. I smile back at her
smile but immediately drop my eyes to my purse, where I pull
out the coins for my purchase. She smiles again, takes the
coins, thanks me – and that's it. I walk out of the shop, ride
my bike back to the beach, stare at the sea and sip my beer.
Negative capability Keats called it: "being in uncertainties,
mysteries, doubts, without any irritable reaching after fact and
reason."

> expatriate
> returning home
> from home

Temps Perdu

Walking past a school in Tokyo. The smell of a cafeteria.
Before I know it, I'm at J. George Becht Elementary, in that
basement room with seasick green walls. The cafeteria. Not
for lunch, but to square dance. Music class. My worst. Boys in
a line on one side; girls on the other. I count. I am better at
mathematics than music, though that is out of tune with
Pythagoras, who insisted that the planets make music as they
move to equations known only to the universe and the soul.

> springtime –
> the pigeons too
> nodding their heads

We are pairing up to square dance and my palms are wet.
Karen Peterson is number nine in the girls' nice straight line. I
am somewhere between seven and ten among the jostling
boys. But I can manipulate numbers. First love. We square the
circle. The dance begins – but soon the spell is broken. My
piriform cortex has let go. Memory, emotion,
metempsychosis, the immortality of death.

Looking back toward the school, I see two pigeons on a wall.
They mate for life.

> park bench
> an old man tugging his beard
> the lovestruck pigeon nods

Cherry Blossoms

Spring has come. The cherry trees are puffed out in pink pride, their blossoms trembling in the breeze over the laughter of the happy family below, enjoying *hanami*, the older ones with their saké and the younger ones squealing for sweets.

Even as the blossoms swell to fullness, the trees lose their grip on the petals, which, one by one and then in clouds, pirouette to the ground, where they lie in scented carpets. Beneath one of these trees, a child with a toy truck scoops a bed of blossoms as he sings a tune about wheels going round and round.

He switches off the video. One of those happy drinkers has passed away. It was so many springs ago he lost that yellow truck. Now he knows why the older ones laughed when they drank, and why, perhaps, they drank.

The pink blossoms are back, and it is *hanami* once again. It won't be long – before the aging trees lose their grip.

> my late mother's birthday
> cherry blossoms
> choke the stream

29

Mother Nature

"O Nature, and O soul of man! how far beyond all utterance
are your linked analogies! not the smallest atom stirs or lives
in matter, but has its cunning duplicate in mind."
— Herman Melville, *Moby Dick*

light on the last leaves
little birds
that stay

crows land
on a slow train
solar eclipse

a bat
in the moonlight
circling its shadow

wind
in high grass
wild horses

morning dew
the little birds
on a rhino's back

dawn
the sea
crawls out of the mist

a path through the woods
all around the silence
invisible eyes

summer holidays
a duck floats backwards
under drowsy willows

wind
in a waterfall
the sun's smithereens

the robin pulls
the worm
pulls back

stubble field
sunset purples
the poplars

a breeze
through wetland reeds
the heron's slow dance

morning breeze
the forefoot of a deer
in a mountain stream

morning
the wetness
under a stone

morning
an egg cracks
from the inside

wolf wind
a fawn sniffs
the dead doe

purple clouds
bursting with thunder
lilacs in the rain

halfway across
the bridge ends
a salmon swims upstream

spring snow
with tiny hands
a mother squirrel lifts a seed

caterpillar
weaving through flowers
the butterfly remembers the way

hunger moon
a crow's beak
in the cat's bowl

turtle eggs
how long it takes
to crawl away

wavering heat
a crow lands
on a high tension wire

pine needles falling in rain heaven scent

honeybee
scented with lilac
fluffing her hair

the sound of silence
looking up at the stars
coyote

ripe barley brushes the sunlight autumn leaves

late autumn
the fields thin
a pheasant's cry

cracked clay
the rhythms of empty corn
in percussions of the sun

shade
splashed with sunlight
blue scented pine

"The creation was an act of mercy."
— William Blake

"There is nothing useless in nature; not even uselessness
itself."
— Michel de Montaigne

"The sky is the daily bread of the eyes."
— Ralph Waldo Emerson

"The flower in the vase still smiles, but no longer laughs."
— Malcolm de Chazal

Once Bereft

What would the world be, once bereft
Of wet and of wildness? Let them be left
　　　— Gerard Manley Hopkins, "Inversnaid"

From Pangaea to the Tethys Sea our Mother Earth goes round, and round our central star appears, the Sun, traveling east to west, from Ethiopia to Hesperides, each day a blessing in this circle of life. Brought into this vital light with plants of every kind and fauna filling land and sea, fruitful, we were. And it was good.

We crept into caves to mark the walls with ochred images of creatures honored for their flesh, their spirit and being, different from our own, yet of the same.

The First Peoples made their homes, dressing their bodies, teaching their tongues, cherishing their kinship with the land.

We learned to turn the very Earth, the oldest of our gods, with plows, back and forth, year after year, reaping, sowing, wearing away the immortal, the seemingly inexhaustible land we would one day forget. And so, as our numbers rose and our cities grew and our knowledge fed our need for power, we tamed and conquered all. Or so we thought we would, quick, ready, resourceful humankind, now more human, less kind, kinship reduced to a great machine.

Our hearts cooled, the Earth warmed, we saw no end in sight. Round and round, each fight, another victory. And then we mastered space itself, we landed on the moon. What sight! The Earth in space – "a tiny, fragile ball of life, hanging in the void." A blue dot where we are all one people, living in one world, together in our need to keep this improbable home home to all creation in all its diversity, its fragile beauty, our one and only home.

Let the earth last
And the forests stand a long time
      — Ayocuan Cuetzpaltzin (a 15th century Aztec poet)

weather satellites
go round and round
empty promises

fracking
we learn new ways
not to change

an electric car
sighs to a stop
the last glacier groans

snowmelt
plum blossoms
on a polar bear

bird of paradise
a rainbow's love song
in a chainsaw repertoire

strip mined
our purple mountain majesties
the emperor's new clothes

old pond
spewing toxic waste
a frog croaks

the caboose
rattles past the setting sun
dust on stunted corn

washing up
on an island paradise
plastic plates

rising tide
she lifts her skirt
to wipe away a tear

a blue balloon
rising into a summer sky
the child waving goodbye

dry riverbed
the old bridge creaks
bone on bone

There is an old Greek word – *homeostasis*, the balance of all
things – which is what we should strive for.

"All things feel."
          — Pythagoras

Song of Myself

"The body is a thing, the soul is also a thing; man is not a
thing, but a drama – his life."
— José Ortega y Gasset

"Man is the only animal that is struck by the difference
between what things are and what they might have been."
— William Hazlitt

the seed promises
the rain gives
man sharpens his blade

alone on a quay
did I miss the boat
or did the boat miss me

open window
a spring breeze
weaves through traffic

summer heat
a damp shirt
on an ironing board

ancient willow
all I know
of the wind

Bamiyan
the rock face
before the mountain was born

after the game
the taste of victory
in the beer

the cold breath
of a thousand strangers
city lights

the last one
leaving the bus . . .
the driver

full moon
a coin in the gutter
almost enough

coins
thrown at wishes
the fountain drains

gazing into my whiskey
a message in a bottle
where a tiny ship should be

sunset
beyond the curve
of the wineglass

evening
voices in the marketplace
soften

greasy spoon
like all the others
I sit alone

Good Samaritan
looking for the child
in everyone he meets

late sunlight
in the monks' deep chant
bumblebees gathering nectar

moonlight
through cherry blossoms
saké shimmers at the brim

raindrops
on an empty beer can
unpaid rent

taking in the sunshine with the laundry

zebra crossing
we move as one
on the way to the zoo

new moon
a reason for being
late

retirement
new wrinkles
in my suntan

morning light
the world stirs
a second cup of tea

spring sunshine
the clean sheets
of perfect strangers

rice field
bent over in summer heat
straw hats

cherry blossoms
she drops a stitch
into the shawl

a dawn wind
wrinkles the sea
mother's voice

rain through city lights
wet stars
winking at our feet

cold fingers
drawing warm milk
the thin cow's baritone

lockdown
the honeysuckle climbs
the garden wall

cloud poem
the mountain lake
the mapmaker missed

a leaf slowly turning past the pilgrim's deep bow

halfway there
the half moon
there

summer breeze
a butterfly quivers
on her fingertip

a solitary cloud
drifts by the setting sun
footprints in wet sand

summer sun
a bugle blares
a single note

anchored in soft sand
an empty boat
tugs toward the setting sun

morning light
gathers in the fishing boats
bougainvillea

an old fisherman
untangles his net
evening's first stars

"The man who goes up in a balloon does not feel as if he were ascending; he only sees the earth sinking deeper below him."
— Arthur Schopenhauer

"Life is the world."
— Ludwig Wittgenstein

The Soul of Wit

"Humor is mankind's greatest blessing."
— Mark Twain

"Good-humor is a philosophic state of mind; it seems to say to Nature that we take her no more seriously than she takes us. I maintain that one should always talk of philosophy with a smile."
— William James

"Humor can get in under the door while seriousness is still fumbling at the handle."
— G.K. Chesterton

"There are things that are so serious that you can only joke about them."
— Werner Heisenberg

"Blessed are the cracked, for they shall let in the light."
— Groucho Marx

clomping through the woods
my only fear
a deaf bear

the writing on the wall
I fear
God is illiterate

fishmonger's slab
all of them
looking at me

Christmas play
the eight-year-old wise man
nibbles his chocolate myrrh

Christmas cheer
boisterous carolers
singing Silent Night

smoking pot
the casserole
almost forgotten

so stoned
epiphanies
blink

taxing year
I cover my losses
with a comb over

acting lesson
you are a pigeon
saying no

moon viewing
waiting for a cloud to pass
the bottle

halloween party
goofy grins
at wonder woman

racing through the intersection
the white-knuckled driving instructor
describes a stop sign

one foot out
of a cheap pair of pants
the mannequin smiles

retirement
forgetting to wait
for the weekend

fishbowl
the tiny gnome at the bottom
waving at the cat

peering through my reflection
the tailor's dummy
with a flower in his lapel

out of luck
a false beard
on my guardian angel

bird feeder
back and forth by the window
the eyes of the cat

locked out
the doorbell
playing ping pong

shadows move across the floor
happily drunk
I moon the moon

old diary
the things I forgot
to do

pet shop
an old parrot eyes
the answering machine

in the last pew
an old man
checks his watch

the emperor's new clothes
Armani
our money

corporations take
a more aggressive stand
glaciers back off

falling stars
the light goes out
on the basement stairs

in the shade
of her sunset asana
a stray dog

hunters
hidden in the shadows
shooting the breeze

dinner selfie
the frozen grin
of the rainbow trout

loosening his tie
the judge reads
the sentence

again
I find myself
contemplating reincarnation

pigeons
hopping about the court
pick-up game

the masked man
no longer
a lone ranger

stand-up comic
with his corny jokes
the audience all ears

each snowflake
a small part
of the cover-up

busking for change
a glove frozen in snow
gives me the finger

proposing
to the nude model
a repose

dark humor
the undertaker
lifts our spirits

the two-year-old
tells granddad all about
dinosaurs

movie of my life
cast and reel
the one that got away

private parts
the gaps in her memoir
a cover-up

luck of the draw
face down on the table
my house of cards

feathers
the memory of a song
in the cat's whiskers

a hare
in a worn hat
the magician combs the ads

millworkers' ball
dancing with the fat guy
in her steel-toed shoes

a bumpy ride
potholes
in my senior year

overdue book
the librarian's horn-rims
moonbeams on ice

credit card
ace in the hole
I dig

hangover
a plastic palm tree
in a tequila sunrise

to be
or knot to be
the alpinist deliberates

unlocked bicycle
the crow on the handlebars
gives me the evil eye

bad outing
the relief pitcher warms up
a can of soup

at the shoe repair counter
a little old lady
on tiptoes

receding wave
the old surfer's
hairline

the wind
passing the dog
through the gate

meteor shower
my wish list
in another coat

food for thought
a claustrophobic astronaut
vacuum packed

what goes around
comes around
hula hoop

a turn for the worst
the brat
at the German barbeque

phony lines
our conversation passes
through pigeon feet

drying out
a rainstorm
scotches my plans

it's legal in some states of mind over matter

the gringo's sombrero
a spaghetti western
dubbed in Japanese

. . . wishing to leave
the riddle of life unsolved,
Buddha smiles.
— Shuntaro Tanikawa

Trailing Clouds of Glory

"There is always one moment in childhood when the door
opens and lets the future in."
— Graham Greene

the dream fades
a zebra finch at dawn
singing to her eggs

summer clouds
a baby bird
in a woman's hands

blue flowers
in a tiny garden
the baby's eyes

the baby's fingers
grasping at her toes
zen circle

mobile
the baby's toes
wiggle above her laughter

the world
before the child
grows into our words

spring rain
a capricious pattering
the toddler's first steps

a pile of shoes
kids at kindergarten
counting their toes

a child
carries a shoe
to his dog

a seashell sings
past golden curls
the child's smile

barefoot
the puppy's little boy
puddles home

a child questions god can't answer

a little boy
shows his pinwheel
to a windmill

a ripe plum
in a child's fingers
sunset

a child
on tiptoes
pointing at a star

summer afternoon
the right fielder
just standing there

four empty swings
sway beneath the trees
mâdadayo

a dog lopes
beside the skipping boy
wild strawberries

sun-bleached façade
the children pack
her unused parasols

cicadas sing
above a child's net
summer ends

a leaf falls
past an open window
first day of school

a shuttlecock
caught in autumn leaves
back to school

wormholes
in the sweetest apples
autumn afternoon

beyond the child's reach
a brown leaf
somersaulting through the park

snow fight
the rat-a-tat-tat
of the children's teeth

spring breeze
restless blossoms
in the teenagers' perfume

her reflection
in a dusty mirror
searchlights in fog

leaves fall
into empty nests
footprints filling with rain

a lamppost leans
on a beam of light
teenage runaway

dry grass
a cricket sings
by the runaway's shoe

bubbles rise
past a sinking stone
childhood dreams

childhood memories
the road leading back
to a one-way street

the ball rolling forever through my little league legs

The Old Country

> morning
> a green apple
> in a child's hands

To sit in an apple tree eating green fruit, hard, sour, cool as the late summer breeze. To remember what I was remembering when I forgot to remember the time, and the sun set behind the barn, and the voices that called me to dinner fell silent.

Where were you!? they scolded when I walked into the weather-beaten old house, the screen door squeaking behind me and the smell of halupki boiling on the stove.

Where was I? Where were we when first we remembered that once we were elsewhere? The Sixth Ancestor asked *Where were you before you were born* and the young monk knew that the apple felt his hands as he held it and knew his tongue when he chewed.

The apples in the pies cooled on the windowsill, as hummingbirds supped on the lilies in the garden. The scent of the pies in the air. Hummingbird wings suffused with the light of the air that we breathe into words. The words of our thoughts. The thoughts of remembering. Green apples.

> forgotten sunlight
> in ripe fruit
> mother's apple pies

Love Is Blind

"The magic of first love is our ignorance that it can ever end."
— Benjamin Disraeli

"The Art of Love: knowing how to combine the temperament
of a vampire with the discretion of an anemone."
— Emil Cioran

"Man is lyrical, woman epic, marriage dramatic."
— Novalis

"If we resist our passions, it is due more to their weakness
than our own strength."
— La Rochefoucauld

new girl at school
his perfect snowball
melting in her hands

bare feet
squelching through mud
our first kiss

a boy and a girl
under a single umbrella
not a cloud in the sky

an eraser
wet with rain
first love

early spring
we take off our gloves
to hold hands

57

pioneer cemetery
two students stop
to kiss

wave upon wave
the hearts of young lovers
drawn in the sand

speaking in tongues
a pretty girl
with an ice cream cone

her dark hair
pulled tight, sunlight
on a wild horse

adam's apple
a lump in the throat
as she covers her breasts

the rest of the night her perfume

spring sunshine
a girl with green eyes
smiles back

fishing together
a little nibble
on her ear

candlelight Chinese
we open up
our fortune cookies

sunrise
the last shadow slips
between her thighs

pregnancy test
true or false . . .
then multiple choice

a little surprise
my girlfriend shows me
a sonogram

corks pop
a happy marriage
no piece of cake

a night breeze
bends the blossomed branch
newlyweds

you smile
I smile
the teapot's piccolo

evening pinks
into night, slowly
she slips off her party dress

kiss me in the middle of the nightingale

a sunny breeze
juggles autumn leaves
loves roller coaster

cat's whiskers
sensing the space
you need

hope springs eternal
in the human breast
her low-cut blouse

bedtime story
I do what fathers do
try to wake my wife

she just doesn't get it . . .
I point at the dog
and then at the stick

faint rumblings
she ponders the sky
beyond his umbrella

storm clouds
the wind
in her dark hair

deep in her eyes the patience of radium

beekeeper:
it's not just me
honey

at her touch
blossoms fall
the fruit small and hard

tight fit
squeezing into the subway
with the woman in jeans

back home
how quickly she removes
her smile

she loves me not
a daisy petal falls
on powdered rhino horn

the sun descends
behind a distant ship . . .
our different horizons

dripping faucet
tedious conversations
we no longer have

at the end of my rope
a stranger at the other end
and a child jumping

after we quarrel
I paint
the doghouse

the hand
that brushed me away
brushing her dog

marriage
on the rocks
another double

lost love
the silence
of a frozen waterfall

the apple of my eye
our office party's Christmas Eve

New Year's Day
a roomful of corks
the genie in my bed

loose thread
that dubious story
about her rumpled dress

the triangle
she plays so well
chamber music

the mirror lies
broken on the floor
picking up where we were

separation
my kit
her caboodle

clean sweep
the broom by the door
reddens in her taillights

her flight departs
that warm sensation
of CO_2

moonlight
in the dumpster
a broken love seat

empty hangers
jangle the wind
dust in her teacup

cooking for one
a little more salt
in the wound

tree stumps
rings for the years
before our separation

a barnacle
on a shipwreck
the divorcee's tattoo

baggage claim
his and hers
the second time around

the billboard model
in her fading underwear
smiles through snowflakes

a billionaire
leaning on his fourth wife
sugar cane

winter blossoms
the elderly couple shiver together
in the shower

"Marriage is a covered dish."
      — Swiss proverb

"Woman was God's *second* mistake."
      — Friedrich Nietzsche

"Bed is the poor man's opera."
      — Italian proverb

The Winter's Tale

winter sun
her shadow follows her
onto the train

an angel
knitting lace
snowflakes

a snowflake falls
on a snowman
faces in a crowd

snowflakes dance
around the hungry sparrows
no two the same

horses steaming
in a field of snow, one by one
the stars

winter night
an old pair of gloves
on the woodpile

a glass of milk
in her unsteady hand
moonlight on a frozen lake

snow flurries
a flutter in the heart
of the waiting room

a tuneless whistling
frets the old man's lips
winter wind

so help me nothing above starlight on snow

starless night
a snow man
with eyes of coal

snow falls
on evergreens
boxes in the attic

friends pass away
snowflakes
melting against the window

winter stars
close enough to touch
her cold hands

epitaph
the stone
beneath the snow

winter rain
the three snow men
kneel as one

late winter
an icicle drips
on an empty mailbox

sunlight on snow
a rabbit sleeps
in the magician's hat

spring snow melts . . .
far from the sea
a marmot sings

Generations of Leaves

Away from books, away from art, the day erased, the lesson
        done,
Thee fully forth emerging, silent, gazing, pondering the
        themes thou lovest best,
Night, sleep, death and the stars.
        — Walt Whitman, "A Clear Midnight"

fresh paint
on the park bench
weathered faces

Chinese New Year
she remembers
the character for home

plum blossoms
on her frail shoulders
a thin shawl

a silent nightingale in her throat cancer

her hair pin
marking the page
on chemotherapy

my aging father
building a birdhouse . . .
his sandpaper voice

golden wrinkles
in an evening sky
mother's smile

second childhood
the setting sun
on a ferris wheel

drought
an old barn
peeling sunlight

a torn dress
covers old bones
she talks to the kitchen wall

the sea roars
in an empty shell
dementia

gnarled fingers
fumble, the candle, by the window
glazed with ice

the last leaf
from a thin branch
spirals toward a frozen pond

dementia
a candle stump sputters
in the pumpkin's empty grin

gravel
at the end of the road
father's voice

a bridge
spanning a frozen river
I sign the DNR

water
on stone
we slip off her wedding ring

at sea
the wind takes possession
of his ashes

the river moves
light from dead stars
past the burning ghats

night falls
through distant stars
into her epitaph

cemetery footpath
the colors of autumn
trod black

spaces
where old pictures hung
water in a net

waves break
over the pier
mother's diary

dad's old trunk
an empty envelope
with a foreign stamp

folded away
behind the empty candy jar
mother's apron

waves rise
and fall into sand
driftwood white as bone

in this universal tragedy
so many
stars

Who are you? A mirror's question never means the same thing
twice; no two *you*'s use that reflection. You too. Two u's in
ululate sing the same one's gone.

Fetch me a stoup of liquor

earthquake
the whiskey shivers
in the judge's hand

a disbelieving rain
falling on stumps
the orphan's small hands

campaign speech
gleaming teeth
chew the air

a plastic ruler
marking a straight line
to the bank

near the white house
the squirrel knows where
to find a nut

feathered sleep
the farmhand's cold fingers
around the chicken's neck

breaking an egg
into the soup
with a chicken bone

life's calculus
the white chalk squeaks
then the eraser

knocking off
a clod from his boot
the gravedigger smiles

candelabra
slowly she loosens the straps
Alhambra

starlight
needles of night
knitting shrouds

It is a graveyard where the plots and the themes of the play
Hamlet converge, and Hamlet is compelled to examine the
nature of life and death. The gravedigger who asks for a
bucket of booze ("fetch me a stoup of liquor") sings and
cracks jokes as he works. He is full of life and at home with
death. He has buried or will bury nearly all the major figures
in the play, as he has buried countless others in his thirty years
on the job. In the end, he will deal with all of us.

leaving forever one day at a time

til death do you part of the deal

the little that matters eventually doesn't it

Not Somewhere Else But Here

A poem asks the reader to participate in the making of its
meaning, and in this way binds the reader to the writer, while
leaving the reader free to bring her own mental associations to
the poet's words and images. Thus, the poem combines a
private and a public language in a process of communication.
While poetry "makes nothing happen" (as Auden stated in his
famous eulogy for Yeats), it can lift the veil from deeply
disturbing aspects of our collective lives and in so doing ask
us to rethink those troubling realties, which we often prefer to
ignore, so long as we feel comfortably secure in our own
personal lives. By engaging individual imaginations, poetry
has the power to bridge the boundaries and divisions that keep
us apart. This is not to say that poetry can improve the world
on a scale that would empower the many millions of
disadvantaged, mistreated, and politically invisible human
beings. But it can help the rest of us to see that these people
exist, and that their sufferings are real, and that we could make
efforts in the real world to ameliorate the condition of their
lives.

the wind picks up
a campaign poster
the hair just right

executive abusio
the warped rule
of blind mouths

wondering which way to turn the nut in charge

a caterpillar
crawls across the evening news
that orange hair

the king of clubs
trumped —
he throws his toys out of the playpen

politics
the ambidextrousness
of a dead bird

day laborer
climbing a ladder
out of the basement

pencil stub
wrinkled fingers pinch
another penny

a cold wind
haggles with golden leaves
savings and loan

a fork
in the road
nothing to eat

the cat lady's eye
strays
each with its own name

a beggar sings
over a coffee tin
nickels counting time

no newspaper coverage
the homeless man
asleep on a bench

a homeless woman
sips from a birdbath
wrinkles in a rainbow

skin
brown and bruised –
the fruit within decays

road sign
rust
in the bullet holes

Peshawar
apples stacked neatly
as the guns

constant drizzle
a faded flag hangs heavy
over another war

fallen
into fallen leaves
toy soldier

crow's feet
around the eyes
sunset on the battlefield

demilitarized zone
the space between
jugglers

the banker's heart as capacious as an open-pit mine

nativity scene
behind an iron gate
the wise men long gone

tree by the wall
a solitary poem
in a life sentence

muddy field
a child in rags
sings to his buffalo

"Unanimity is almost always an indication of servitude."
— Charles de Rémusat

"Resist the times: offend popular sentiments."
— Lu Xun

"Patriotism is the last refuge of a scoundrel."
— Dr. Samuel Johnson

"Burning stakes do not lighten the darkness."
— Stanislaus Lec

"For the merchant, even honesty is a financial speculation."
— Charles Baudelaire

Help

light
imprisoned in diamonds
the dark mine a dollar a day

windblown sand –
children in rags
staring as the boat recedes

orphans at the stoplight
together
we roll up our windows

winter
a bent spoon
in an empty pot

shoe polish
the toxic smell
of unemployment

a few stars
fewer leaves
his cardboard home

a rainbow ribbon
on a rich man's sky
tree stumps

outside the new megastore
empty shopping carts
for the homeless

yesterday's snow
under a naked tree
a homeless woman awaiting spring

old nails squeaking
in shrinking wood
campaign promises

the populist's campaign
a loud speaker
distorts the platitudes

air raid
our last loaf of bread
blackens in the oven

a child's balloon
drifts away
the wall crowned with broken bottles

Human rights encompasses a great deal. As stated in the
Preamble to the United Nations' Universal Declaration of
Human Rights: "recognition of the inherent dignity and of the
equal and inalienable rights of all members of the human
family is the foundation of freedom, justice and peace in the
world." Extreme inequality has profound human rights
implications. Nearly 10% of the world's population lives in
extreme poverty, and over 40% live on less than $5.50 per
day, thus depriving those members of the human family access
to basic needs and services.

A Paper Bird

Perhaps the self-same song that found a path
   Through the sad heart of Ruth
      — John Keats, "Ode to a Nightingale"

The aunt who always bought me presents I didn't like. Wool
sweaters. It's a Pendleton, she would say. *How to* books. You
can never know too much, Baby Bob, she insisted – though I
was thirteen.

I wrote an essay about her in high school, an exercise in
metaphor and symbol.

Childless, divorced, she lived alone. When I left town, I
promised to write. I never did – though one day I drew a little
bird by her address to remind me that I should.

        summer leaf fall
        a postcard
        to the wrong address

One day a letter arrived. Aunt Ruth had passed away. I put an
olive leaf in the bird's beak.

        dusty closet
        some pretty wrapping paper
        and an empty box

Birdsong

Drunk birds slur their songs. That we have learned, boozing finches far beyond their wintered berries.[1]

How birds resemble ourselves. The anthropologist Claude Lévi-Strauss noted that, "like us, birds love freedom and they build themselves homes in which they live a family life and nurture their young." Literature is rich with metaphorical bird communities. Aristophanes showed that life is for *The Birds*, and Chaucer had Nature teach the importance of free will to a *Parliament of Fowls*.

Since ancient times, the songs of birds, pouring forth their tuneful souls, have inspired musicians and poets. Some have even speculated that human music, our universal language, has its origins in birdsong. We make music because it sounds beautiful to our ears, and we use it not only for enjoyment but also to celebrate important events.

> day begins
> the voice of a nightingale
> imprisoned in the violin

The French composer Olivier Messiaen was fascinated with the connections between music made by humans and that of birds. As a prisoner in a Nazi concentration camp he composed his *Abyss of the Birds*, eight movements of astonishingly beautiful music, where the instruments weave in and out of their harmonies, rhythms, and chords to rise up toward a heavenly end. In the living hell of the camp, his winged spirit brought together the sonic enthusiasm of birds with the long, dark weight of eternity. In his notes to the piece, he wrote: "The birds are the opposite of time. They represent our longing for light, for stars, for rainbows, and for jubilant song. In my hours of gloom, when I am suddenly aware of my own futility, when every musical idiom – classical, oriental, ancient, modern and ultramodern – appears to me as no more than admirable painstaking experimentation without any ultimate justification, what is left for me but to seek out the true, lost face of music somewhere off in the forest, in the fields, in the mountains or on the seas, among the birds."[2]

With winged words Walt Whitman sang that the poet should learn his music from the mockingbird. In such a way, the German artist Kurt Schwitters turned the songs of birds into his famous sound poem *Ursonate*. The poet's song may take flight and transcend mundane life, allowing anyone who makes that song their own, by giving to its syllables their breath, a means to rise above the sullen earth and like the lark sing hymns at heaven's gate.

> sunlight on water
> vowels
> in the syllables of birds

Why do birds sing? Their songs keep flock and family together; they unite pairs in the spirit of love; they teach the young. Their music is essential to their survival. Humans share with birds the ability to learn to sing.

> baby finches hunger for their father's songs

And yet we put birds in cages. As Shelley sang of one young woman: "Poor captive bird! who, from thy narrow cage, / Pourest such music, that it might assuage / The rugged hearts of those who prisoned thee, / Were they not deaf to all sweet melody." And as the poet Paul Laurence Dunbar sang of black Americans: "I know why the caged bird sings." He was singing for the freedom that is the natural province of the bird, as it is for all human beings.

> music repeats
> the uncaged melody
> a beak between the bars

Notes:

1. Studies show that drunk birds slur when they sing. In an effort to gain insight into how alcohol affects the cognitive functioning of birds, researchers gave spiked fruit juice to

zebra finches, who consumed the tasty beverage until they were well and truly hammered, after which they began to sing, clearly slurring their songs. The same sort of thing happens in nature. Bohemian waxwings, for example, get tipsy on fermented berries, which can cause them to fly into windows and walls. Good Samaritans that they are, the environment department in the Yukon, in Canada, has set up avian drunk tanks, where wasted waxwings, with their red-stained beaks, can sober up before they fly off into spring.

2. The French avant-garde composer Olivier Messiaen was one of most distinctive voices in 20th century music. He had been fascinated with the connections between music made by humans and that of birds since his teenage years. During the early years of World War II, he was a prisoner in the Nazi concentration camp Stalag 8A, which held over 30,000 people. The Red Cross gave him music paper and identified a few other musicians in the camp, and they secured a few violins, cellos, clarinets, and a single piano. There, he completed one of his most celebrated compositions, *Abyss of the Birds*, the first of many to feature the sounds of birds. In the first movement, the clarinet and violin trade sounds from blackbird and nightingale, and the solo clarinet third movement is an attempt to link the endless enthusiasm of singing birds with the long, dark weight of eternity.

For a Muse of Fire

"Drawing is taking a line for a walk."
— Paul Klee

"The object of art is to give shape to life."
— Jean Anouilh

" . . . give me
the exact name of things!
. . . I want my word to be
the thing itself"
— Juan Ramón Jiménez

"Only through art can we emerge from ourselves and know
what another person sees."
— Marcel Proust

"Thank you for letting me read your new poems. It was like
being alive twice."
— Li Po (in a letter to Tu Fu)

a parrot
in a peepal tree
the painter lifts his brush

a painter's touch
she draws me
water from a well

in an unfurnished room
she stands naked
the light touch of the painter's brush

weeping willows
brush the pond
she paints to forget

autumn leaves
an unfinished painting
in a rusty dumpster

a blue breeze
summer passes slowly
on an old guitar

late sunlight
sweeps the woodland
chords on an old guitar

a grace note
in a familiar song
early autumn

autumn leaves
my son plays
my old guitar

busking at Christmas
a battered guitar
reflects a star

the blue between
rain clouds
cool jazz

summer evening
through thin curtains
cool jazz

jazz solo
the deep blue
of a winter sky

whiskey sour notes through a dented sax

her willowy frame
smoke
through a saxophone

dusk
lighting her almond eyes
oboe d'amore

flowerbed
my lover on a summer day
dressed in song

foghorn
a barge glides by
the oompah band

noh chanting
covering their faces
the tourists yawn

music store window
beyond my reflection
the score for a requiem

kindergarten choir
children in and out of tune
the melody in their eyes

night shift
gliding a broom across the floor
an émigré waltzes

the sandpiper's cuneiform
translated
in the poetry of waves

sunlight through icicles
an old watercolor
falls from her scrapbook

Ob-La-Di, Ob-La-Da

The songwriter sits by still waters. So many have come before.

Come, muse, and take my hand from the rod. Drop a line into
my pallid score. Clear my mind of the numberless others, put
paid to the Fabulous Four.

> fishing
> for the right lyrics
> earworm

Apsara

O body swayed to music, O brightening glance,
How can we know the dancer from the dance?
        — William Butler Yeats, "Among School Children"

The rainy season has begun. Irises are blooming around the small pond in the park. Around the purple flowers around the moss green pond elderly painters – amateurs in the loving sense of that word – have taken out their easels, their brushes, their watercolors, and, shoulder to shoulder, begun to capture the scene.

I smile as I move behind them, each painting blossoming into life, fraternal twins, triplets, quintuplets, one harmonious family of canvases of purple irises around a dark rain-spotted pond.

Among the circle of female aquarellists is an elderly man, his easel, brushes, watercolors set in their places between his partners in paint beside the flowers, the water, the silent harmonizing.

I smile as I stop behind him. His canvas owes nothing to the purple irises or the moss green pond. He is painting the figure of a dancer, a divine apsara, youthful, ethereal, one with her dance.

The painters to his right and to his left are unswayed, as are the flowers, the pond, the rain. He paints and his dancer moves with his brush, and, as we do, I pass away.

           Leonardo mixing paint
           the eye
           before the smile

Enter time . . . an imaginary garage

Surrealism aims to release the creative powers of the unconscious mind. Central to the surrealistic method is the use of strange, even bizarre, imagery to reveal the more mysterious aspects of living.

I do not see surrealism in terms of a surrender to the irrational but rather as a means of altering conditioned perspectives as a means of rediscovering the delights of uncommodified experience, in a dance with the imagination. The writer coaxes from her words a bemused witness to the weirdness of the world.

Reverie and paradox can mystify the mind so that it relaxes and receives messages and meanings that retain their mystery and wonder. Unconventional associations of language and thought can be liberating in the sense that nonsense may allow one to put in her two cents without fear of being overcharged. To astonish, surprise, bewilder, perplex and sometimes boggle the mind. To see the world anew, whirled before the eyes, of which each one has two. Exit, pursued by a bear.

"Language is always a little ahead of our thought, has a higher boiling point than our love."
    — Gaston Bachelard

"There is a fine line between fishing and just standing on the shore like an idiot."
    — Steven Wright

"There is another world, but, it is this one."
    — Paul Éluard

"Black holes are where God divided by zero."
    — Albert Einstein

enter time, a chorus of wasp waisted silhouettes

I park my Ferrari
in an imaginary garage
crickets click in the locks

nebulae of gnats talk radio

dawn
curdled cream
in the pigeon's coos

bonsai
the canary sings
on cue

the pendulum swings
cuckoos improvise
the end of time

a cross
black cats
the path

a nutshell
in infinite space
bones of an ancient beast

waves
moonwalk
whale song

a ghost
in the machine
writing a wild horse

eyesight dims
threading a needle
on camelback

a hole in the prairie dog moon

icicles melting
over wildflowers
wolves teeth

taxidermist
the end game
stares back

ribs
eaten by the wind
the sun bleeds away

a clown slips
into his smile
crescent moon

swollen eyes
in the damp moonlight
the potato dreams

stargazing
how small they seem, each
with two bright eyes

jewel thief
in the middle of the night
falling stars

money poisoning my well enough alone

space probe circling pluto
a small coin
to the boatman

blood moon
hanging from an olive tree
the last of the wine

icicle moon
a doe-eyed maiden
on a black stallion

undressing
an imaginative construct
in real time

the spring
of a pogo stick
mud luscious

winged soprano
coming
wet with night

girlie bar
the broken plumbing
in a pigeon's love song

the city at night
a necklace of windows
tightening at my throat

the fractured self
a ventriloquist's dummy
bites his tongue

wind wailing
through ancient trees
the chainsaw's clenched teeth

talking to myself
the stigma
of self-pollination

cyclone
a naked doll
with one blue eye

el nino
the boy next door
throwing snowballs at our roses

lightning
a skeleton riverbed
opens her arms

windswept clouds our thinking scud missiles

whistling past the graveyard shells

Liberty Bell
the crack that holds
its iron tongue

vodka and sauerkraut
a thick mist settles
a border dispute

final filibuster
the hourglass fills
with formaldehyde

water drifts
under thin ice
the surgeon's blue eyes

earthquake
the old cathedral
waves a finger at the sky

black summer
knights a knave
rising with sea-blue stars

a thirsty insect
wiggles in the wine
the ethics of salvation

the axe sticks
in the green wood
infantile amnesia

time salts our pulled hare

lollipop babel
a baby rainbow
too sleepy to cry

farmhands at noon
asleep by the hen house
sunny side up

dead fish
in a dented bucket
life on Mars

thin men
with frightened hair
cloves

haunted graveyard
a summer breeze
unzips the grass

lonely   i
wise men   magi
together   nation

a north wind blows the alley cat round the corner

please william tell of the boy beneath the apple

heat wave
he winds the spring
until it snaps

a ninja
wearing a cowbell
climate change

toothache
an alarm clock
made of glass

Modraniht. Tears freeze over grave dew. Snowflakes wrestle
the avalanche. Drunk fish sleep beneath a diamond sky
wedded to the water's cheated lutz. An axel breaks the wheel
of life.

Semantics

God is dead, or, strictly speaking, *Gott ist tot*, declared the German philosopher Friedrich Nietzsche. He didn't mean dead like lying in a pool of blood in a dark alley, shell casings circling a rusty drain. No. More like missing in action, or just plain gone – long after the statute of limitations has run out and the paperwork has been filed and the cleverer relatives have found a way to collect on His, or Her, insurance policy. Dog-gone!

Death: To be ... lifeless; bereft of sensation or vitality; benumbed; insensible. The bucket kicked; the ghost given up; the dreamless sleep pushing up daisies.

Dead is seldom said. We prefer the deceased, the dear departed, the testator or testatrix. Strange, that there are so many words for beneficiary and just one or two, mostly unknown ones too, for the giver of beneficence. We prefer passing away. Into a realm where tomorrow's dreams awake into yesterday's television programs we can watch on YouTube.

I can't help but wonder. What would YouTube have been called were it a French invention? Would they use the familiar form – such that we would be watching TuTube? Or the formal form – VousTube, which I suppose sounds a bit too much like voodoo?

But we started with God. And God is formless, or so, at least, was the earth when God said *Let there be light*, which, one may presume, He did not do lightly. Or She – but what matter, if God is formless? The light was separated from the darkness, which tells us that God did not create the heavens and the earth at the North Pole in midsummer, though He, or She, might have done, finding it particularly difficult to sleep. That is what too much enlightenment can do.

> in failing light
> bent over a battered board
> checkmate

The Book

In June of 1977, I handed to a friend, as he boarded a plane that would carry him from Pakistan to his home in Australia, discouraged from further travels by a recent illness, my copy of Henry Miller's *Plexus*, inside the green tattered cover of which I had written a few words. That was the last I saw of my former traveling companion.

I stayed on the road, traveling onward to India, Nepal, Sri Lanka, Thailand, and eventually to Japan, where I settled for a year and met the woman who would later become my wife, and with whom I left Tokyo in the spring of 1979 to return to India and Nepal. In October of that year, I dropped into a bookstore on Freak Street in Kathmandu to peruse the offerings for something to read as we trekked to the original Everest Base Camp at Gorak Shep and back, a two-month adventure requiring a couple of very thick books.

Looking along the shelves, I spotted the green spine of a rather hefty, and strangely familiar, book. When I leaned in closer, I could see the title – *Plexus*, by Henry Miller. A wave of nostalgia washed over me. I remembered reading the very same novel on my journey through Central Asia, and finally passing it on to my departing friend. I took the volume from the shelf and opened it at random, then flipped through the pages. Strange, very strange. The book not only looked familiar, but felt familiar.

I closed the book, and then turned back the front cover. Impossible. There were the words I had written, in a book that had been carried to Sydney, Australia, two and half years earlier, in the hands of a person who had never, I was sure, ventured from home again. What should I do with this mysterious literary talisman?

In the end, I ignored the urge to possess the book again, sensing that it would be more appropriate to leave it on the shelf in that little bookstore in Kathmandu, where another traveler could find it and take it with him or her on another journey, different from my own.

each step begins a journey
diverging from another
the lives we leave behind

To Professor Kenneth Woodroofe, who clarified for me that life was for living. And to my wife Aiko, who has lived it with me. And my children, Layla and Alex, and my grandchildren, Kai and Mina, and my friends, and my mother and father and brother and sister, and the beauty of the world we must leave for all.

In the end, there would be peace.

Robert Witmer lives in Tokyo, Japan, where he has resided for the past 45 years. He has published poems and works of prose in many print and online journals. His first book of haiku, *Finding a Way*, is available on Amazon and from the publisher, Cyberwit.net.

Made in United States
Troutdale, OR
04/15/2024

19195130R00063